RACE THROUGH ROME

TIMOTHY KNAPMAN

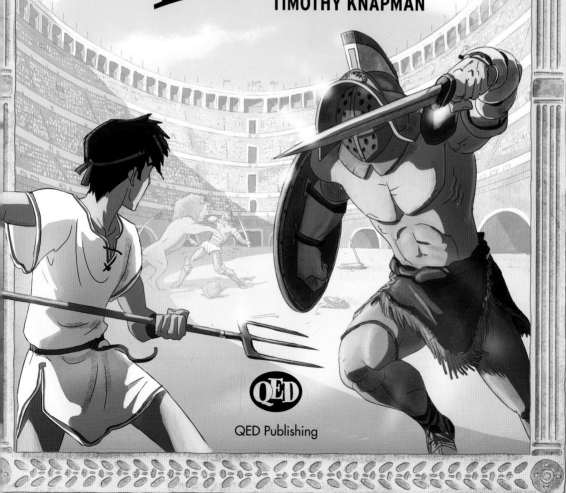

QED

QED Publishing

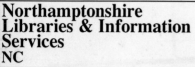
Cover Design: Punch Bowl Design
Illustrator: Matteo Pincelli
Editor: Amanda Askew
Designer: Andrew Crowson

QED Project Editor: Ruth Symons
Managing Editor: Victoria Garrard
Design Manager: Anna Lubecka

First published in the UK in 2013 by
QED Publishing
A Quarto Group company
230 City Road
London EC1V 2TT

www.qed-publishing.co.uk

A catalogue record for this book is available from the British Library.

ISBN 978 1 78171 146 0

Printed in China

Picture credits
Shutterstock: Danilo Ascione, 9, 23; Marcel Nijhuis, 33; superdi, 43

How to begin your adventure

Are you ready for an amazing adventure in which you must face deadly foes, survive terrible dangers and solve fiendish puzzles? Then you've come to the right place!

Race Through Rome isn't an ordinary book – you don't read the pages in order, 1, 2, 3... Instead you jump forwards and backwards through the book as you face a series of challenges. Sometimes you may lose your way, but the story will always guide you back to where you need to be.

The story begins on page 4, and soon there are questions to answer and puzzles to solve. Choose which answer you think is correct. For example:

IF YOU THINK THE CORRECT ANSWER IS A, GO TO PAGE 37   **IF YOU THINK THE CORRECT ANSWER IS B, GO TO PAGE 13**

If you think the correct answer is A, turn to page 37 and look for the same symbol in red. That's where you will find the next part of the story.

If you make the wrong choice, the text will explain where you went wrong and let you have another go.

The problems in this book are about life in ancient Rome. To solve them, you must use your history knowledge, as well as common sense. To help you, there's a glossary of useful words at the back of the book, starting on page 44.

Are you ready?
Turn the page and let your adventure begin!

WELCOME TO
ROME

You arrive in ancient Rome on a day of great celebration. The Emperor is having a Triumph: a magnificent parade to celebrate his latest victory in war. It's your dream to meet him, but it won't be easy.

To succeed, you'll need to keep your wits about you. Are you ready for the quest?

GO TO PAGE 19
TO START YOUR ADVENTURE!

The wooden sword is called a *rudis*.

It was given to a gladiator who had been so successful he was given his freedom.

Lucius lets you go. He suggests you stay to watch the games. But you don't have a ticket or any money.

What do you do?

JUST WALK IN AND HOPE YOU'RE NOT SPOTTED. **GO TO** PAGE 26

STEAL A TICKET. **GO TO** PAGE 37

Roman feasts were as much about showing off as eating.

The pig isn't there as food.

GO BACK TO PAGE 17 AND THINK AGAIN

Good idea! You're standing next to a public lavatory, and a sponge on a stick is what Romans use to wipe their bottoms!

One look at that and the thief runs away. You've torn your clothes in the chase and need new ones. Time to go shopping!

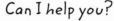

Can I help you?

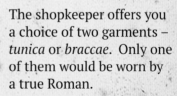

The shopkeeper offers you a choice of two garments – *tunica* or *braccae*. Only one of them would be worn by a true Roman.

Which do you choose?

TUNICA. **FLIP TO** PAGE 37

BRACCAE. **GO TO** PAGE 36

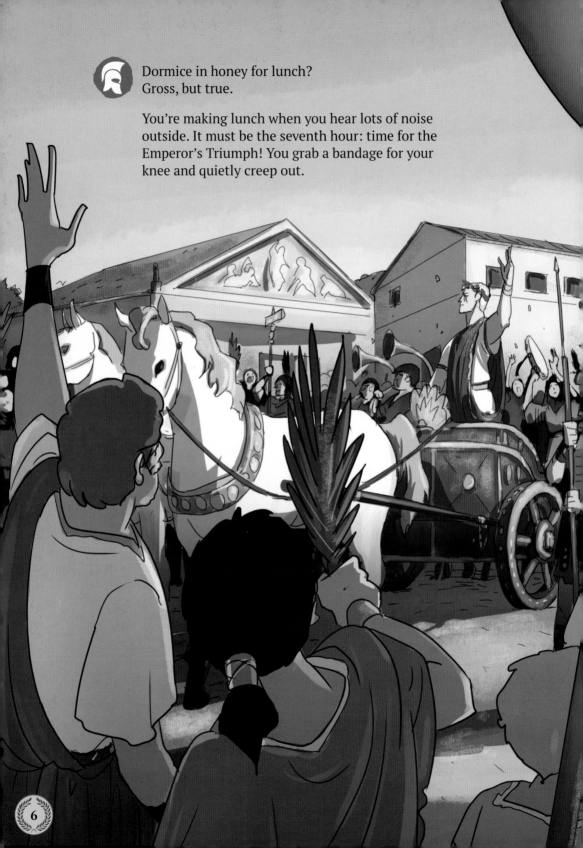

Dormice in honey for lunch?
Gross, but true.

You're making lunch when you hear lots of noise outside. It must be the seventh hour: time for the Emperor's Triumph! You grab a bandage for your knee and quietly creep out.

There are cheering crowds everywhere. The parade is led by the senators. Then there are trumpeters, carts stacked with loot, the enemy leaders in chains – and finally the Emperor himself.

You want to get a better view, but there are too many people in the way.

You look around. What can you grab that will help you get through?

A KNIFE.
GO TO
PAGE 26

A BUNDLE OF RODS WITH AN AXE BLADE.
GO TO PAGE 12

A FRUIT CART.
TURN TO
PAGE 37

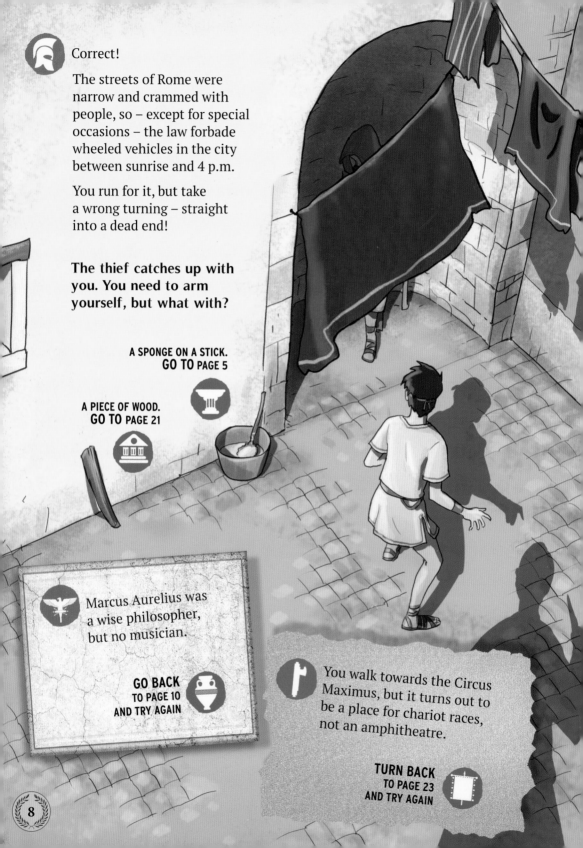

Correct!

The streets of Rome were narrow and crammed with people, so – except for special occasions – the law forbade wheeled vehicles in the city between sunrise and 4 p.m.

You run for it, but take a wrong turning – straight into a dead end!

The thief catches up with you. You need to arm yourself, but what with?

A SPONGE ON A STICK.
GO TO PAGE 5

A PIECE OF WOOD.
GO TO PAGE 21

Marcus Aurelius was a wise philosopher, but no musician.

GO BACK
TO PAGE 10
AND TRY AGAIN

You walk towards the Circus Maximus, but it turns out to be a place for chariot races, not an amphitheatre.

TURN BACK
TO PAGE 23
AND TRY AGAIN

Although it sounds like a place to be sick, the *vomitorium* is a wide passageway for crowds to leave the building quickly.

You're back on the streets. You nearly forgot about the Emperor's parade, so you ask a passing Roman what time the Triumph starts.

He replies, *"At the seventh hour."*

The Romans counted the hours forwards from sunrise (6 a.m.). So what time does the parade start?

AT 12 P.M.
GO TO
PAGE 10

AT 1 P.M.
SKIP TO
PAGE 42

AT 2 P.M.
TURN TO
PAGE 19

There are plenty of statues of men on horseback around, but that's not right.

GO BACK
TO PAGE 19
AND TRY AGAIN

The blue line shows the Empire in 100 BCE – it was going to get bigger than that!

GO BACK
TO PAGE 36

That's right. Caligula made his favourite horse, Incitatus, a senator.

Hmph, the senators don't even smile before asking:

"Question 2: Which emperor played music while he watched Rome burn?"

NERO.
GO TO
PAGE 36

MARCUS AURELIUS.
TURN TO
PAGE 8

 The kitchen, or *culina*, was dark and smoky because it had no chimney. It's no place to wait for your new friend.

GO BACK
TO PAGE 28
AND TRY AGAIN

 If you arrive at 12 p.m. – or noon – you'll be an hour early.

GO BACK
TO PAGE 9
AND TRY AGAIN

60–80 is the right number.
The soldier lets you pass.

There's only one set of armour
left – a legionary's – but there are
three helmets to choose from.

Which one is a legionary's helmet?

IF YOU THINK IT'S
THIS HELMET,
GO TO PAGE 27

IF YOU THINK THIS IS
THE RIGHT HELMET,
GO TO PAGE 16

IF YOU THINK THIS
HELMET MATCHES,
GO TO PAGE 30

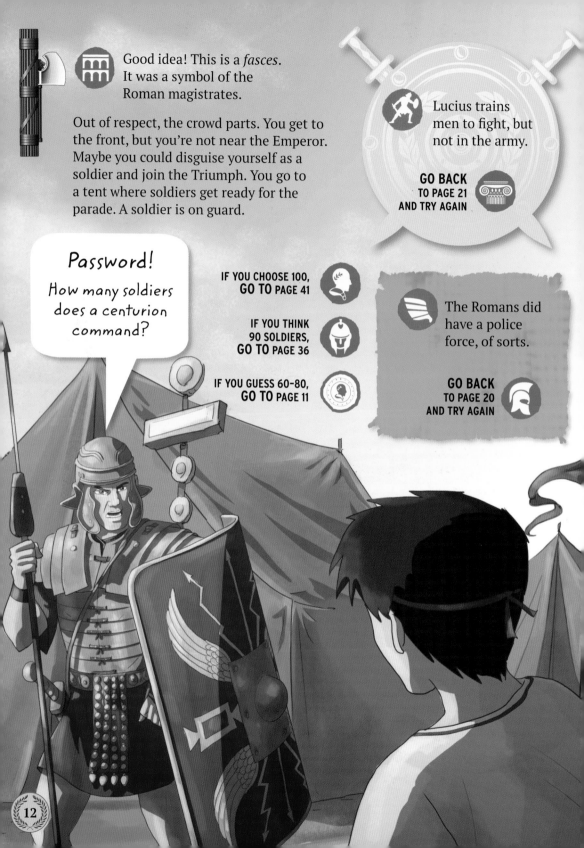

Good idea! This is a *fasces*. It was a symbol of the Roman magistrates.

Out of respect, the crowd parts. You get to the front, but you're not near the Emperor. Maybe you could disguise yourself as a soldier and join the Triumph. You go to a tent where soldiers get ready for the parade. A soldier is on guard.

Lucius trains men to fight, but not in the army.

GO BACK
TO PAGE 21
AND TRY AGAIN

Password!

How many soldiers does a centurion command?

IF YOU CHOOSE 100,
GO TO PAGE 41

IF YOU THINK
90 SOLDIERS,
GO TO PAGE 36

IF YOU GUESS 60-80,
GO TO PAGE 11

The Romans did have a police force, of sorts.

GO BACK
TO PAGE 20
AND TRY AGAIN

No, the Roman word for wild boar is *aper*.

GO BACK TO PAGE 14 AND TRY AGAIN

The Roman Empire did not include the whole of Africa!

GO BACK TO PAGE 36 AND TRY AGAIN

 ...and the Emperor thinks that you have saved his life!

Guards! After those men!

The guards chase the thieves through the crowds. To thank you, the Emperor wants to make you a senator. The snobby senators think you are too ordinary and want you to answer a series of questions before they'll agree with the Emperor.

"Question 1: What animal did the mad Emperor Caligula make a senator?"

HIS DOG. **GO TO** PAGE 28

HIS HORSE. **GO TO** PAGE 10

 After walking for a while, you sit on a wall for a rest, next to a young boy. You notice a sign nearby that says

CAVE CANEM.

"I'm just visiting. Is Cave Canem a good place to go?" you ask the boy.

With a mischievous smile, the boy says you must a play a game of dice with him before he tells you. The dice have Roman numbers on them. The boy then asks:

"Which score is higher?"

THE BOY'S. **GO TO** PAGE 28

YOURS. **GO TO** PAGE 41

That's right!

You can see bears, lions and other wild animals in the arena.

There are trapdoors around the arena. If you move quickly, you can escape through the one behind Leo.

Animals and gladiators are fighting all around you.

Who or what is Leo?

THE GLADIATOR. GO TO PAGE 37

THE WILD BOAR.
GO TO PAGE 13

THE LION.
GO TO PAGE 22

An eagle is correct. It was sacred to Jupiter, king of the gods, and represented power. Phew!

There's a great eagle statue on the arch that leads to the market square.

"Hmm. Maybe that was too easy. Try this one. What is the meaning of the letters SPQR written underneath the eagle?"

SPQR

IS IT THE NOISE
AN EAGLE MAKES?
GO TO PAGE 37

IS IT THE ROMAN
SENATE AND PEOPLE?
TURN TO PAGE 20

No, that's a centurion's helmet.

GO BACK TO
**PAGE 11 AND CHOOSE
ANOTHER HELMET**

I stands for one.

GO BACK TO
**PAGE 29
AND THINK AGAIN**

 The gladiator with a net and trident is a *retiarius*.

He just throws his net over you! You breathe a huge sigh of relief.

You're brave and clever. You could last a long time as a gladiator and make lots of money. I don't want to let you go, but I tricked you into coming here, so I will give you a chance to escape. Choose one of these swords — one is a symbol of freedom but the other will seal your fate as a gladiator!

Which one do you choose?

THE WOODEN SWORD. **GO TO** PAGE 5

THE RAZOR-SHARP STEEL SWORD. **GO TO** PAGE 28

 The *frigidarium* is the cold room. Your chattering teeth will give you away in there.

GO BACK TO PAGE 34 AND THINK AGAIN

18

The first place you come to is a busy street market.

People are selling all sorts of things, including food, spices and clothes.

Out of the corner of your eye, you see a man stealing money from a stall.

"*Stop! Thief!*" you shout. There's a scuffle and the stallholder grabs the thief.

Then everyone turns to look at you, and the stallholder speaks.

If you arrive at 2 p.m., you'll be an hour late and you'll miss the Triumph.

GO BACK
TO PAGE 9
AND DO THE
SUM AGAIN

Door A stands between Vulcan, the god of fire, and Mars, the god of war, and underneath Neptune, the god of the sea – so it's locked!

QUICKLY, GO BACK
TO PAGE 32
AND THINK AGAIN

You are a stranger. You must be working with this thief! Prove that you are loyal to Rome by answering my questions.

What is the great symbol of Rome?

Think carefully. Is it:

AN EAGLE.
JUMP TO PAGE 16

A SNAKE.
FLIP TO PAGE 27

A HORSE.
TURN TO PAGE 9

That's right!

SPQR stands for *Senatus Populusque Romanus*, which is Latin for 'the Roman Senate and People'.

The stallholder nods and lets you go.

Just then, the thief breaks free and runs for it.

You wonder why the stallholder doesn't call for the police.

What could be the reason?

THERE WASN'T A
POLICE FORCE.
GO TO PAGE 12

THE POLICE FORCE FOUGHT FIRES
RATHER THAN CRIME.
TURN TO PAGE 31

THE POLICE DIDN'T BOTHER
WITH SUCH PETTY CRIMES.
JUMP TO PAGE 43

Romans didn't use
soap to get clean.

TRY AGAIN
ON PAGE 42

Some bathhouses had reading rooms, but handing out books wasn't the *capsarius*'s responsibility.

GO BACK
TO PAGE 43
AND THINK AGAIN

The thief has a
dagger. He isn't
scared of a piece
of wood.

**THINK AGAIN AND
TURN BACK TO PAGE 8**

 That's correct!

The Emperor laughs and invites
you to tonight's feast.

You are beaming! You have fulfilled
your quest – not only have you met
the Emperor, you're having dinner
with him!

**YOU TRAVEL WITH
THE EMPEROR TO HIS
PALACE ON PAGE 17**

 X is 10, quite right – and there is
Lucius, waiting for you.

There are two large men with him. Lucius
tells you that they are enrolled at his *ludus*.
You ask Lucius what type of school it is.

I know you're clever, so you
can work it out. I train men for
events held at this amphitheatre.
They need to be strong.

What type of school is it?

**A SCHOOL FOR
OUTSTANDING ATHLETES?
GO TO PAGE 33**

**A TRAINING SCHOOL
FOR FIGHTERS CALLED
GLADIATORS?
TURN TO PAGE 24**

**A SCHOOL FOR ROMAN
SOLDIERS?
FLIP TO PAGE 12**

That's right! *Leo* is the Roman word for lion.

You dodge behind the lion and jump through the trapdoor before it closes.

Under the arena, there are lots of passageways and tunnels and you get lost.

You reach two doorways.
Which one do you go through?

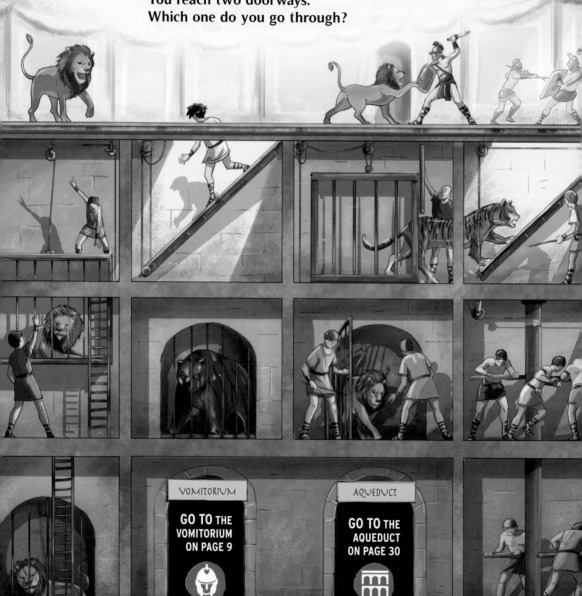

VOMITORIUM

GO TO THE VOMITORIUM ON PAGE 9

AQUEDUCT

GO TO THE AQUEDUCT ON PAGE 30

 That's right. You find the central hall, where the boy is waiting with a drink.

"What a fantastic room! Great skylight! But where are the windows?"

The boy laughs. You'll have to work it out for yourself.

THERE WAS A TAX ON WINDOWS. GO TO PAGE 36

ROMANS WEREN'T GOOD AT GLASS-MAKING. GO TO PAGE 42

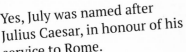 Yes, July was named after Julius Caesar, in honour of his service to Rome.

The bookseller gives you the book – and the thief wanders past without noticing you.

It's probably time to meet Lucius at the amphitheatre.

You see a sign. Which way do you go?

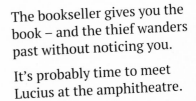

TO THE COLOSSEUM ON PAGE 29

TO THE CIRCUS MAXIMUS ON PAGE 8

 The *caldarium* is the hot room. The thieves will easily spot you there.

GO BACK TO PAGE 34 AND THINK AGAIN

That's right, *ludus* is short for *ludus gladiatorius*, which means gladiator school!

No need to worry. It's easy, really. Come and have a go. But be warned — only the *retiarius* will spare your life this time...

Lucius hands you a dagger.

You are faced with three fearsome-looking gladiators.

So which gladiator do you attack?

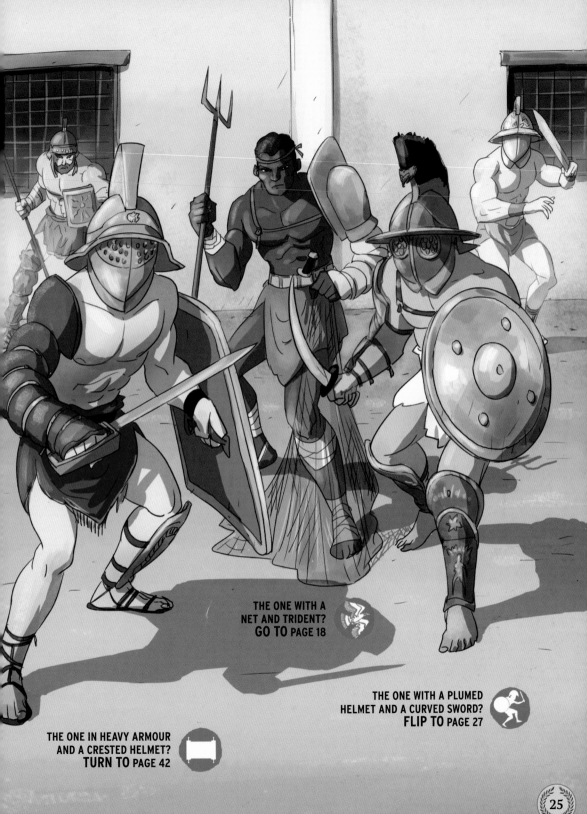

THE ONE WITH A
NET AND TRIDENT?
GO TO PAGE 18

THE ONE WITH A PLUMED
HELMET AND A CURVED SWORD?
FLIP TO PAGE 27

THE ONE IN HEAVY ARMOUR
AND A CRESTED HELMET?
TURN TO PAGE 42

You just walk in. The games were free to enter, paid for by rich Romans who wanted to show off their wealth or win support.

You take your seat, but someone in the crowd has recognized you – it's the thief! He pushes his way towards you, looking very angry. You ask the man next to you for help.

> We're about to watch a venatio. If you can tell me what that is, I'll show you how to escape.

How do you answer?

IT'S A WILD ANIMAL HUNT.
GO TO PAGE 14

I LOVE A SEA BATTLE.
TURN TO PAGE 43

OF COURSE, IT'S A
GLADIATOR FIGHT.
GO TO PAGE 31

If you wave a knife, people will think you're trying to attack the Emperor.

GO BACK
TO PAGE 7
AND THINK AGAIN

The Romans dug trenches to defend their army camps, but not their borders.

GO BACK
TO PAGE 37
AND TRY AGAIN

Yes, that's right!

You join the legion. The Emperor emerges and the crowd cheers. You wave your helmet in celebration – but the thief and his friends are in the crowd. They move towards you with daggers in their hands!

You run backwards, bumping into the imperial party. The Emperor looks at the thieves, and at you...

**GO TO
PAGE 13
TO FIND OUT
YOUR FATE**

 The gladiator in a plumed helmet with a curved sword is a *thracian*.

That sword is sharp!

GO BACK TO PAGE 25
**AND PICK ANOTHER
GLADIATOR QUICKLY!**

 Snakes symbolized many things in ancient Rome, including eternal life, but the snake is not the symbol of Rome.

**GO BACK
TO PAGE 19
AND TRY AGAIN**

Yes, the boy has rolled IV+V+III (4+5+3), so his score is 12 and is higher than yours. The boy tells you that the sign means 'Beware of the Dog'.

It's probably not the best place to visit!

"Would you like a drink? My house isn't far," says the boy.

You nod and he takes you to his house. *"I'll get the drinks. Wait for me in the atrium."*

What is an atrium?

THE CENTRAL HALL.
GO TO PAGE 23

THE DINING ROOM.
GO TO PAGE 30

THE KITCHEN.
GO TO PAGE 10

CAVE CANEM

You picked the steel sword?

You're going to need it, as you'll be spending the rest of your life (which may not be long) fighting gladiators.

A dog?
Don't be crazy!

GO BACK
TO PAGE 13
AND THINK AGAIN

QUICK, **GO BACK**
TO PAGE 18
AND CHOOSE
AGAIN!

28

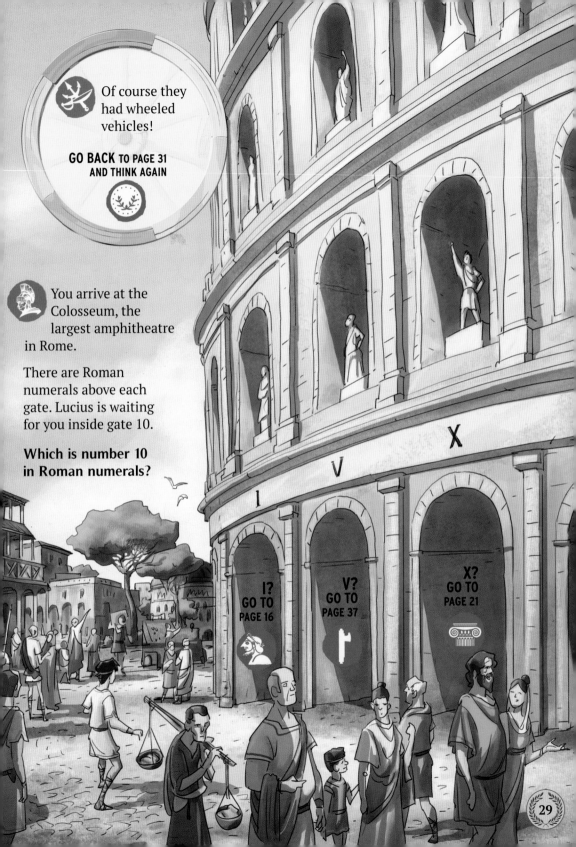

Of course they had wheeled vehicles!

GO BACK TO PAGE 31 AND THINK AGAIN

You arrive at the Colosseum, the largest amphitheatre in Rome.

There are Roman numerals above each gate. Lucius is waiting for you inside gate 10.

Which is number 10 in Roman numerals?

I V X

I? GO TO PAGE 16

V? GO TO PAGE 37

X? GO TO PAGE 21

The dining room is called the *triclinium*, which means the room of three couches. That's because Romans ate dinner lying on couches.

GO BACK TO PAGE 28 AND TRY AGAIN

 No – that's a cavalryman's helmet.

GO BACK TO PAGE 11 AND CHOOSE ANOTHER HELMET

 No, the *aqueduct* is the channel for water. It is used to flood the amphitheatre for a sea battle.

GET BACK TO PAGE 22 AND CHOOSE AGAIN

 No that's the medicine table. The Romans thought garlic was good for the heart, sage would help the gods heal you, fennel calmed the nerves and boiled liver soothed the eyes.

GO BACK TO PAGE 40 AND TRY AGAIN

Correct! Emperor Augustus formed a sort of police force called the *vigiles*, but they spent most of the daytime putting out fires.

This was important in a city of wooden buildings – and that's why the *vigiles* could only fight crime after dark.

You walk away from the market and feel like someone is following you. It's the thief – and he looks angry!

If only you could jump aboard a passing vehicle, but why can't you find one?

THE ROMANS DIDN'T HAVE WHEELED VEHICLES. **GO TO** PAGE 29

WHEELED VEHICLES WERE NOT ALLOWED IN THE CITY. **TURN TO** PAGE 8

Fights between gladiators weren't the only shows put on in amphitheatres.

GO BACK
TO PAGE 26
AND TRY AGAIN

31

NEPTUNE

CUPID

APOLLO

VENUS

A

B

MARS

MINERVA

VULCAN

JUPITER

 The building is a temple!

Maybe the priest will know a way out.
But he gives you a riddle:

"If you choose the path between fire and war and go under the sea, you will find the way blocked. It is the path between wisdom and the king, under the eye of love, that leads to freedom."

You realize this means a route marked by statues of the gods. Can you find the right path out of the temple?

IF YOU CHOOSE DOOR A,
GO TO PAGE 19

IF YOU CHOOSE DOOR B,
GO TO PAGE 41

 Correct!

You can still visit the remains of Hadrian's Wall in northern Britain.

The man pays for your clothes.

> My name is Lucius. I run a *ludus* — a kind of school. Someone as clever as you could go far there. Meet me at the amphitheatre, gate 10, in two hours.

Before you have a chance to ask what the amphitheatre is, he's gone! You'd better start exploring the city.

GET STARTED
ON PAGE 13

 There would be slaves to clean up after you, but a *capsarius* wasn't one of them.

GO BACK
TO PAGE 43
AND THINK AGAIN

 You have to be fit to join a *ludus*, but it's not a school for athletes.

GO BACK
TO PAGE 21
AND THINK AGAIN

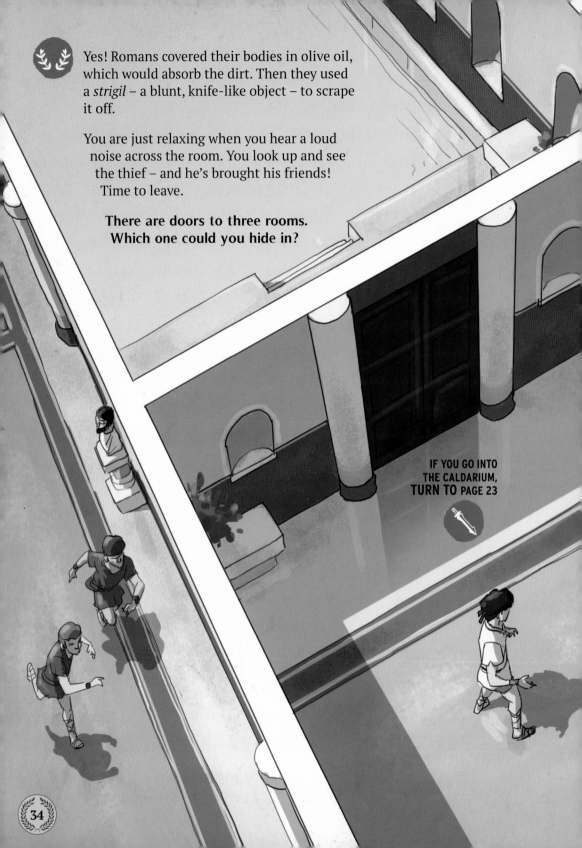

Yes! Romans covered their bodies in olive oil, which would absorb the dirt. Then they used a *strigil* – a blunt, knife-like object – to scrape it off.

You are just relaxing when you hear a loud noise across the room. You look up and see the thief – and he's brought his friends! Time to leave.

There are doors to three rooms. Which one could you hide in?

IF YOU GO INTO THE CALDARIUM, **TURN TO** PAGE 23

IF THE
FRIGIDARIUM
SOUNDS RIGHT,
GO TO PAGE 18

IF YOU FANCY
THE SUDATORIUM,
FLIP TO PAGE 43

The Romans taxed many things – including unmarried men – but not windows.

GO BACK TO PAGE 23 AND TRY AGAIN

 Braccae are trousers – and Romans didn't wear them. They thought anyone who did was a barbarian (a crude foreigner).

IF YOU'RE GOING TO FIT IN, **GO BACK** TO PAGE 5 AND PICK SOMETHING ELSE

 90 is too many.

TRY AGAIN ON PAGE 12

 Nero, a mad emperor, thought he was a great artist, and played his lyre while the Great Fire of Rome destroyed the city.

The senators look cross that you're on your way to being one of them!

"Your final – killer – question… Question 3: The Empire has never been bigger than it is now in 117 CE. But which line shows the border of the Empire today?"

THE BLUE LINE? **GO TO** PAGE 9

THE RED LINE? **GO TO** PAGE 21

THE GREEN LINE? **GO TO** PAGE 13

The shopkeeper hands you the *tunica*, or tunic, the garment every Roman wore.

Oh no! You have no Roman money. You're in big trouble now...

Another customer has entered the shop and saves your skin!

"Wait! I'll pay — if the youngster can answer my question: In north Britain, there is something that keeps Roman enemies out of the Empire. What is it?"

A DEEP TRENCH.
GO TO PAGE 26

A GREAT WALL.
JUMP TO PAGE 33

 Romans aren't stupid. Nothing could make such an odd noise!

GO BACK
TO PAGE 16
AND TRY AGAIN

 V stands for five.

GO BACK
TO PAGE 29
AND THINK AGAIN

  No, he's there to control Leo!

GO BACK
TO PAGE 14
AND TRY AGAIN BEFORE
YOU GET EATEN!

 People might move out of the way of a fruit cart, but not that quickly.

CHOOSE AGAIN
ON PAGE 7

 You'll have a problem stealing a ticket because you didn't need one to get into the games!

GO BACK TO PAGE 5
AND CHOOSE AGAIN

 The Colosseum was built by Emperor Vespasian and his sons more than a hundred years after Julius Caesar died.

GO BACK TO PAGE 41
AND THINK AGAIN

Of course not!

You know it's for decoration only. One of the slaves pulls out a sword and cuts the pig in half. A flock of song thrushes flies out of the pig and everyone around the table applauds.

At the end of the meal, the Emperor says you are a true Roman and bids you good night.

You have succeeded in your Roman quest: you have met the Emperor – and, better still, you've stayed alive!

 You're right! Clothes being stolen from the changing rooms was a common problem.

You leave the baths. When you slipped over, you cut your knee. Lucky for you, next to the baths is the shop of a *medicus*, or doctor.

He's busy treating a patient so he doesn't look round at you. *"Finally! Make my lunch now!"* he orders.

He must think you're a slave. You look at the tables.

Which is the dinner table?

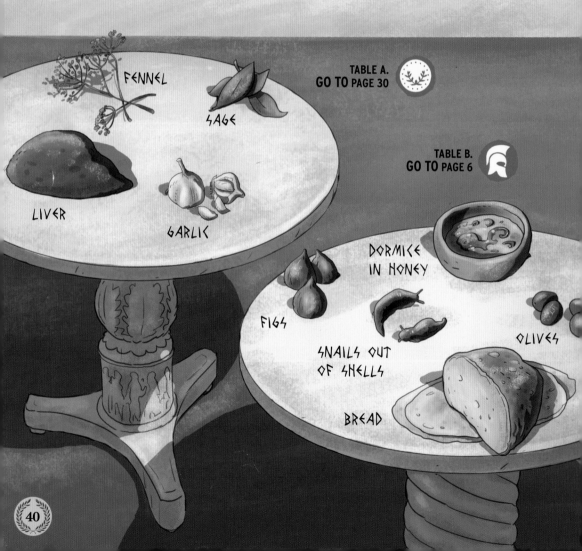

FENNEL

SAGE

TABLE A.
GO TO PAGE 30

TABLE B.
GO TO PAGE 6

LIVER

GARLIC

DORMICE
IN HONEY

FIGS

SNAILS OUT
OF SHELLS

OLIVES

BREAD

Door B stands between Minerva, goddess of wisdom, and Jupiter, king of the gods, and underneath Venus, the goddess of love – that's the way out!

Outside, there's a large stall selling rolls of papyrus – Roman books. You pick one up to hide behind.

Excellent. You must be learning about the great Julius Caesar. Tell me something you've learned about him and you can keep that book.

You don't want to draw attention to yourself while the thief is around, so think hard.

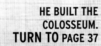 THE MONTH OF JULY IS NAMED AFTER HIM.
GO TO PAGE 23

 HE BUILT THE COLOSSEUM.
TURN TO PAGE 37

 No, you rolled VI+II+I (6+2+1), so you scored 9. That's not higher than the boy's score.

The boy tells you that Cave Canem is a great place to visit... But when you get near it, a guard dog starts barking!

YOU'D BETTER **TRY AGAIN** ON PAGE 13

 Even though *centum* was the Roman word for 100, centurions didn't command that many men.

GO BACK TO PAGE 12 AND PICK ANOTHER ANSWER

That's right! The Romans couldn't make clear glass, so they didn't have windows in their houses.

You thank the boy for the drink and leave to find the amphitheatre.

You round a corner and in front of you is a large beautiful building. Is this the amphitheatre? There's a man standing nearby – you're sure he'll know.

As you get closer, you realize the man is actually the thief. And he's spotted you!

RUN INTO THE BUILDING
ON PAGE 32

The gladiator in heavy armour and a crested helmet is a *murmillo*. He's a champion and has killed many men.

GO BACK
TO PAGE 25
AND PICK ANOTHER
GLADIATOR QUICKLY!

 That's right.

Seven hours after 6 a.m. is 1 p.m. – the seventh hour. Only one hour away!

You're quite grubby and need a wash before you try to meet the Emperor, so you head towards the public baths.

Inside the baths, a slave approaches you with perfume, a towel and a strangely-shaped tool.

But what's missing?

SOAP.
GO TO PAGE 20

OLIVE OIL.
TURN TO PAGE 34

The *sudatorium* is the steam room. The steam is so thick that you can hide under their noses!

You sit down and relax... and fall asleep! You wake up with a start – have you missed the parade?!

You run into the changing room, but slip over on the wet floor and send a slave flying.

This slave is called a *capsarius*. He has a very special job in the Roman baths, but what is it?

HE GUARDS THE CLOTHES IN
THE CHANGING ROOMS.
GO TO PAGE 40

HE COLLECTS THE
DIRTY TOWELS.
TURN TO PAGE 33

HE LENDS BOOKS TO
PEOPLE IN THE BATHS.
GO TO PAGE 20
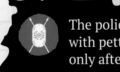

The police did deal with petty crimes, but only after dark.

GIVE IT ANOTHER
GO ON PAGE 20

Amphitheatres could be flooded, and great sea battles fought in them, but this wasn't called a *venatio*.

GO BACK
TO PAGE 26
AND TRY AGAIN

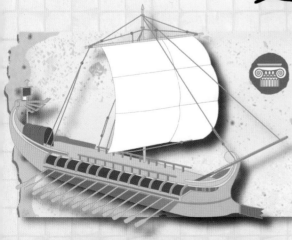

Glossary

Amphitheatre
A large oval or circular open-air venue for gladiator fights and wild animal hunts. An amphitheatre could also be flooded to stage sea battles, or *naumachia*. The most famous amphitheatre is the Colosseum in Rome.

Aqueduct
A channel or bridge that carried water from one place to another. In ancient Rome, aqueducts brought water to the cities and towns.

Atrium
A large open space inside a building.

Barbarian
A person who did not embrace the Roman way of life.

Caldarium
A hot room at the Roman baths.

Capsarius
A slave at the baths who guarded the changing rooms to stop thieves stealing the clothes.

Centurion
A soldier who commanded 60–80 legionaries.

Circus Maximus

A huge sporting stadium in Rome for 150,000 spectators. Athletic competitions, gladiator fights and theatre performances were staged there – but it was most famous for chariot races.

Colosseum

The large amphitheatre in Rome where gladiator fights were held. It seated 50,000 spectators. It was the largest amphitheatre in the world.

Emperor

The ruler of Rome and its Empire. The first Roman emperor was Augustus, who ruled 27 BCE–14 CE.

Empire

The lands and peoples ruled by the Romans. At its largest – during the reign of the Emperor Trajan (98–117 CE) – it covered 5 million square kilometres and had 60 million inhabitants. In 395 CE, the Empire split in two – the Western Empire governed by Rome, and the Eastern by Constantinople (modern-day Istanbul).

Frigidarium

A cold room at the Roman baths.

Gladiators

Male or female slaves who fought each other – sometimes to the death – for public entertainment. There were many different types – each with different armour and weapons. Gladiators were usually slaves, criminals or prisoners of war. They could sometimes win their freedom if they became successful fighters.

Hadrian's Wall
Built by Emperor Hadrian (reigned 117–138 CE) to mark the northern border of the Empire, and keep out the dangerous barbarian tribes that lived in what is now Scotland.

Latin
The language of the ancient Romans, spoken throughout the Empire.

Legion
The Roman army was made up of legions, each with 5000 foot soldiers, called legionaries. Roman soldiers were fiercely loyal to their legion and would fight to the death to protect it.

Ludus
A training school for gladiators.

Magistrate
A judge in a court of law.

Murmillo
A gladiator with a crested helmet who wore heavy armour.

Philosopher
Someone who studies the meaning of life.

Retarius
A gladiator who carried a net and a trident.

Rudis
A wooden sword given to a gladiator who had been so successful that he was given his freedom.

Senator
A rich, powerful Roman who was part of the senate. Under the Roman Republic, the senate made the laws. When emperors took over, the senate lost most of its power.

Slave
A person owned by another person, who had to do what they were told all day long.

Sudatorium
The steam room at the Roman baths.

Temple
A building where people go to worship their god or gods.

Thracian
A gladiator with a curved sword who wore a plumed helmet.

Triumph
A parade to celebrate the emperor's latest war victory.

Tunic
A simple item of clothing worn by most Romans. Men wore knee-length tunics and women wore floor-length tunics.

Venatio
A wild animal hunt staged at an amphitheatre for entertainment.

Vomitorium
A wide passageway in an amphitheatre by which crowds could leave the stadium quickly.

Taking it further

The History Quest books are designed to inspire children to develop and apply their historical knowledge through compelling adventure stories. In each story, readers must solve a series of historical problems to progress towards the exciting conclusion.

The books do not follow a page-by-page pattern. The reader jumps forwards and backwards through the book according to the answers given to the problems. If their answers are correct, the reader progresses to the next part of the story; incorrect answers are fully explained before the reader is directed back to attempt the problem once again. Additional help may be found in the glossary at the back of the book.

To support the development of your child's historical knowledge you can:

- Read the book with your child.

- Solve the initial problems and discover how the book works.

- Continue reading with your child until he or she is using the book confidently, following the 'Go to' instructions to the next puzzle or explanation.

- Encourage your child to read on alone. Prompt your child to tell you how the story is developing, and what problems they have solved.

- Point out the differences and similarities of life in Roman times compared with life today – what we wear, eat and do for fun.

- Discuss what it would be like if an ancient Roman visited us today. Or if we went back in time to the ancient city.

- Take advantage of the many sources of historical information – libraries, museums and documentaries. The Internet is another valuable resource, and there is plenty of material specially aimed at children. Take care only to visit websites endorsed by respected educational authorities, such as museums and universities.

- Remember, we learn most when we're enjoying ourselves, so make history fun!